Loren Kaye

MAYFAIR
EXPOSED

SYLPH
EDITIONS

Mayfair Exposed

I HAVE LIVED IN MAYFAIR for many years. This central London neighbourhood has a long-standing reputation for wealth and glamour, conjuring images of fur coats and gleaming Rolls-Royces. It was only during the pandemic, however, when I began to carry a camera during long roaming walks, that another Mayfair opened up to me: the Mayfair of ordinary people, both residents of local social housing and people who come in every day to work in the shops, hotels and galleries.

My camera became a tool that enabled me to strike up conversations with my unknown neighbours. A photographic project began to emerge that attempted a more expansive view of Mayfair, showing both its exposed and underexposed sides. I asked people to allow me to take their picture, but also looked afresh at the streets through the lens of my camera. Through this focused exploration, this place – about which I thought everything had been said – acquired new depth and complexity.

Mayfair, as shown in *Stanford's Map of London and suburbs*, 1862

It was important to me to portray both the affluent public face of Mayfair and this quiet, multifaceted world within a world – with a clear emphasis on the second. I wanted to see and show, but how would people react to the woman with the camera, asking to take their picture? Some answered with a resounding no; others granted me easy trust; others still extended their trust more cautiously. With the exception of the resolute no's, the photographs in this book cover every shade.

In Mayfair, two worlds sit side by side. One world is out in the open, on permanent display, overexposed, as it were; the other is all but invisible. Though they occupy the same small area of London, they hardly touch, gliding past one another in an uncanny frictionless way. 'Would you ever have spoken to me if it hadn't been for your camera?' Latifa, a resident of a historic Mayfair social housing block, asked me. I had to respond with a sobering 'no'. Through this book, I hope in some small, personal way to redress this omission. A flip of the switch, a click of the shutter: a change in perspective which I know, for me, is permanent.

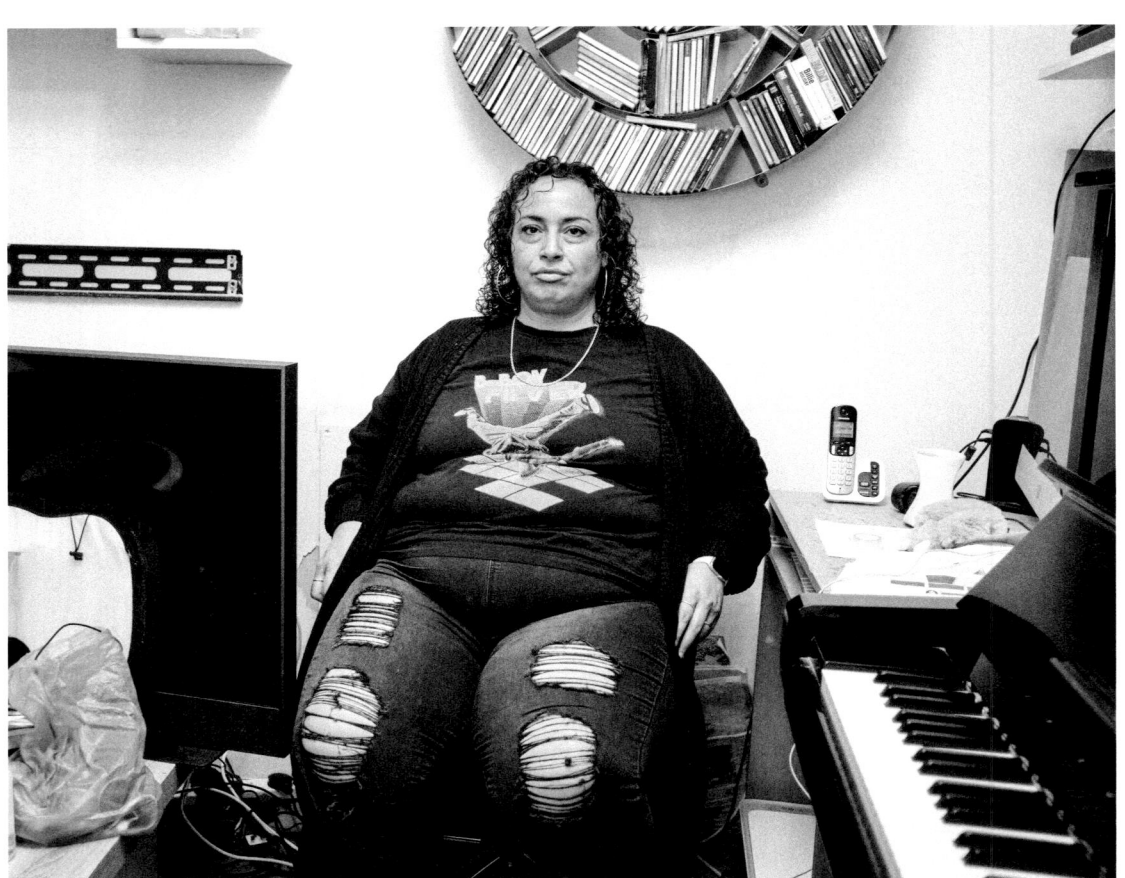

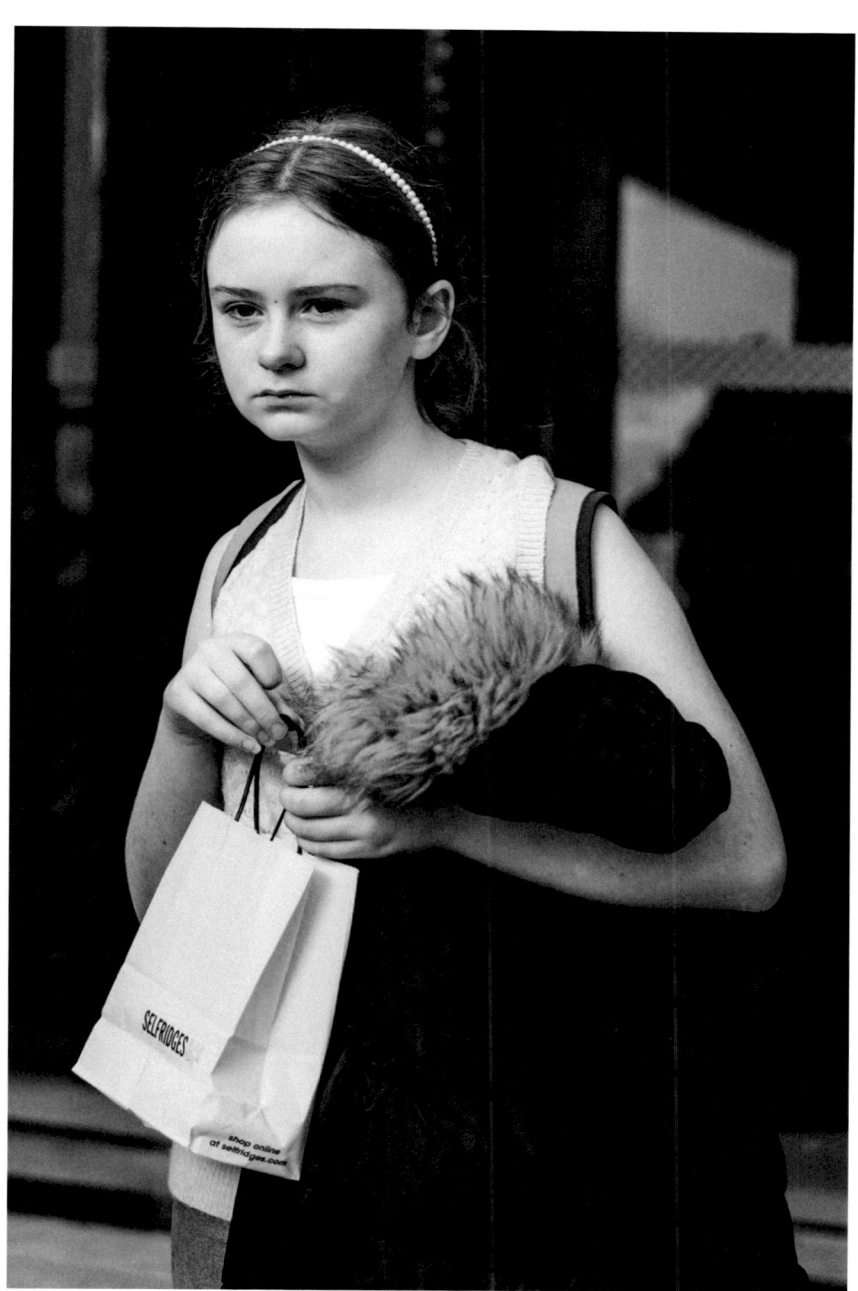

Some reflections on Mayfair, its past and present

THE PEOPLE I GOT TO KNOW as part of this project are a diverse group. They are taxi drivers and estate agents, chambermaids and antiques dealers; they are shop assistants and wealthy shoppers. I took pictures of local schoolchildren and retirees, people who had been living or working in Mayfair for decades and people just passing through, people with all sorts of cultural backgrounds. I spoke to homeless people and those who live in some of the capital's most expensive, coveted flats.

    Over the course of my exploration, I forged a particular connection with a few residents of Mayfair's little-known social housing blocks. These blocks of flats mainly occupy a small grid of streets in north-west Mayfair, just south of Oxford Street and bordered to the east by Davies Street. They are stately, six-storey red-brick buildings, built in the late 19th century as part of a social housing initiative by the stupendously wealthy Grosvenor Estate, which owns a large portion of prime Mayfair real estate to this day. Today the buildings are administered by the Peabody housing association on behalf of Westminster council. This community is hidden in plain sight, with the buildings' restrained Gothic style allowing them to blend in well among their more opulent neighbours.

Another historic block is found a little further to the southeast on Bourdon Street, near Berkeley Square with its high-end art galleries. Known as the St George's Buildings, it was built in 1853 on the initiative of the local parish and remains reserved for social renters today. This former mews area was home to many working-class people in the 19th century; on Bourdon Street, a row of beautiful historic stable and coach houses remains.

Through my conversations with residents, I became aware of how deeply rooted many of them are in Mayfair. It is far from easy to get a social flat in Westminster; in 2024, the waiting list for a two-bedroom flat is ten years. However, under certain circumstances it is possible to 'inherit' a tenancy from a family member. In this way, some families have occupied the same flat for generations.

I photographed Latifa in her flat at her piano. She played from Chopin's *Nocturnes*. She has lived in Mayfair for 27 years and loves the parks, the buildings, the local library and cinema and the excellent transport links. But, she says, Mayfair has its challenges: there is little in the way of food options for people on average or lower budgets, so one has to go elsewhere to shop or eat out. She noted that the people range from the very rich to the poor. Roma beg on the streets, drunks keep you up at night singing or shouting. Shops dazzle with goods you can't buy, languages from all around the world buzz in your ears.

Mayfair has a well-regarded Church of England state primary school, St George's, which makes the neighbourhood attractive to young parents – a 'godsend' as one mother called it. The blocks near Oxford Street all have micro-gardens on the rooftops allotted to the tenants, affording them some respite from the relentless bustle below. Regent Hall, the nearby Salvation Army centre, provides inexpensive entertainment by renowned symphony orchestras.

Over the last 20 years, these residents have watched the neighbourhood undergo sweeping changes. These are changes I have witnessed myself with a growing sense of ambivalence. Mayfair has become a place oriented towards the outside – specifically, towards the wealth it can attract from investors, tourists and shoppers. Mount Street, once a sleepy side road with a forlorn post office, antiques stores and a 200-year-old butcher, is now populated by wannabe fashionistas who sit outside café hotspots and queue to acquire luxury brands. Menacing sports cars, imported for the season, roar past, bellies low to the ground. This part of Mayfair became known as 'Little Doha' after the Qatari ruling family started buying up huge swaths of local real estate in the early 2000s. The embassies, formerly a mainstay of the area, have moved out and have been replaced by high-end, exorbitantly priced apartments and ultra-luxe hotels. Mayfair's historic village-like atmosphere has been displaced by a ubiquitous display of aggressive consumerism, leaving a void at the centre of the neighbourhood.

Nigel, the concierge at the renowned Claridge's hotel, sees these changes in the context of his 40-year career at the hotel. From a professional point of view, he says, Mayfair has been experiencing what he calls a renaissance. In the last ten years, many Michelin-starred restaurants and fashionable stores have opened. Claridge's has spent huge sums on upgrading the hotel for the 21st century. Nigel feels that Mayfair has always been cosmopolitan. He told me a little of its history and showed me the trace of the underground River Tyburn, which starts in Hampstead Heath and makes its way down the hill across Oxford Street and along Avery Row next to Claridge's, then under Buckingham Palace before merging with the Thames.

And indeed, pockets of tranquillity remain amid Mayfair's rush to transform with the times. Mayfair's elegant historic squares – Grosvenor, Hanover and Berkeley – offer expansive lawns ringed with beautiful plane trees. The largest, Grosvenor Square, is overlooked by the former US Embassy building designed by the modernist Eero Saarinen in 1960. Further east, on fashionable Bond Street, one can admire the Time & Life Building with its integrated Henry Moore sculptures. Three prominent churches, Anglican, Catholic and Ukrainian Orthodox, have deep roots in the area. 'Living in Mayfair', commented Ray, a long-time resident of the Peabody flats, 'is exciting and unreal; a privilege, but draining.'

One of my goals with this book is to show that Mayfair is a place both of sharp contrasts and subtler shades. The residents of Mayfair's social housing and its incoming workforce are very well aware of its social complexity. 'I live on the charity side of Mayfair,' observed Derek, another long-time resident. Another local, Bronwyn, generally doesn't tell people she lives in Mayfair as it comes with too many assumptions: 'People judge me differently and then they're disappointed.' These experiences are absent in the portrayal of Mayfair in the culture at large. It is my hope that this book will add some of these missing gradations to the image of Mayfair by portraying the range of individuals who live and work in this singular slice of central London.

For further information about the project and about the history of Mayfair's social housing, see the book's website at www.mayfair-exposed.art

COLOPHON

ACKNOWLEDGEMENTS

I would to thank all the people who were willing to share their Mayfair with me: Agushev, Andra, Anna, Boris, Bronwyn, Calvin, Carl, Carlos, Cass, Christina, Christopher, Dara, Dave, Derek, Dr Nazeer, Gordon, Graham, Harry, Helen, Jan, Janus, Jean Clare, Jermain, Joseph, Kitty, Latifa, Leo, Maggie, Mark, Misha, Mr Bodie, Mr Rowley, Nigel, Pat, Paula, Peter, Peter, Ralph, Ray, Raymond, Robin, Sylvia, Tariq, Tarun, the children and parents from St George's C E Primary School, Shirley, Tommy's Boyz, and, lastly, those who preferred to keep their names to themselves.

Special thanks to Christopher Giglio and Jim Grover.

All images in the book were taken over a period of three years, between January 2021 and December 2023.

© LOREN KAYE, 2024

No part of this publication may be reproduced in any form whatsoever without the prior written permission of the photographer or the publisher.

Editorial: Mona Gainer-Salim

Design: Ornan Rotem
    Set in Trinté by Bram de Does, a typeface rooted in the works of the 20th-century Dutch typographer Jan van Krimpen and in forms prevalent in Italian Renaissance calligraphy.

Printed and bound in Amsterdam by robstolk®
    Text on Symbol Tatami and cover in Sirio Pearl Oyster

SYLPH EDITIONS

London · 2024

ISBN 978-1-909631-45-8
www.sylpheditions.com